KOLAH
THE KOALA

TRUE-TO-LIFE BOOKS
Educating children about endangered species

Photographed by Jan Davis, Jon Resnick and George Apostolidis

Written by Jon Resnick

Designed and produced by Jan Davis

Koala Books

Hi, my name is Kolah and I'm a koala.
I live in Australia where my ancestors
have lived for over 15 million years.

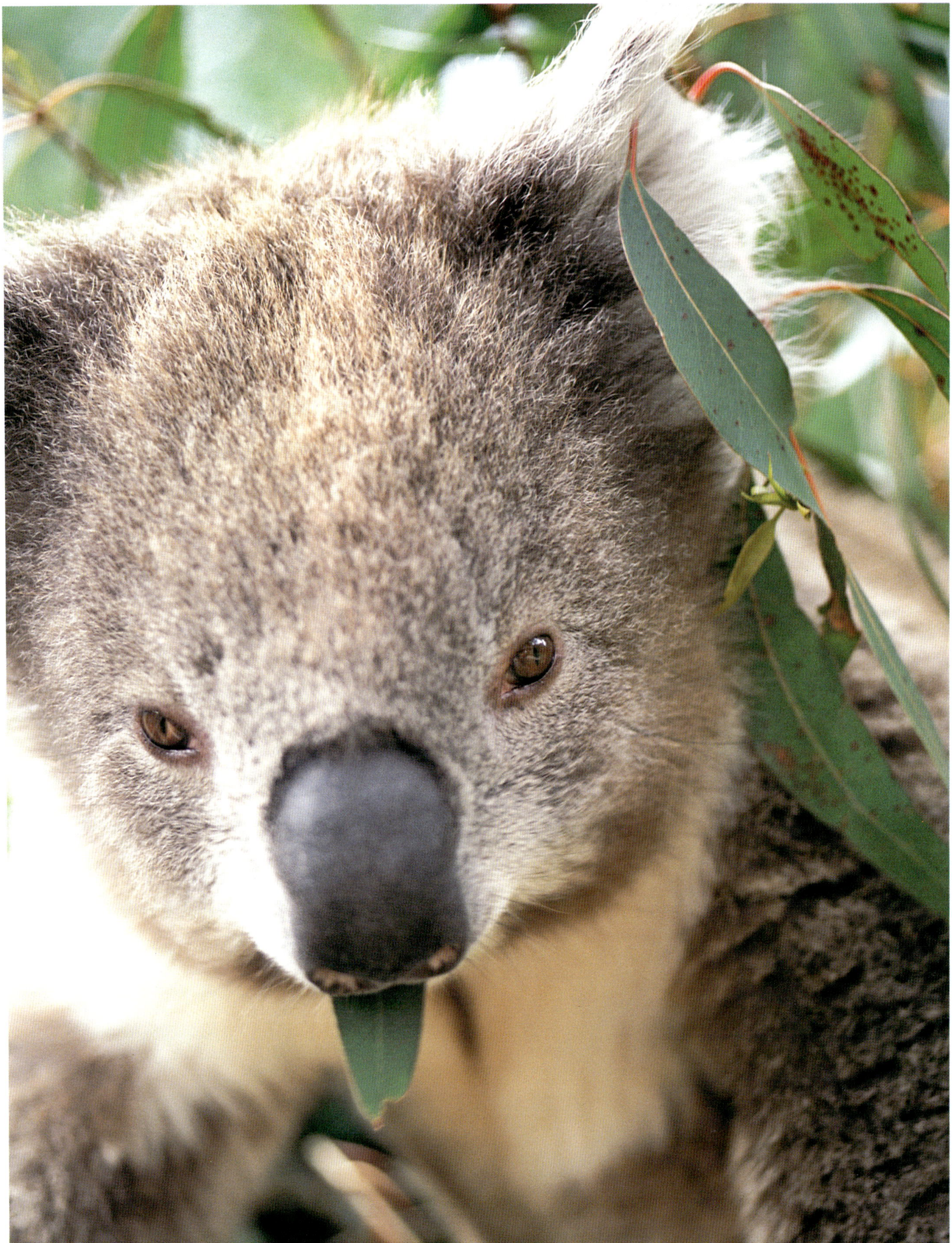

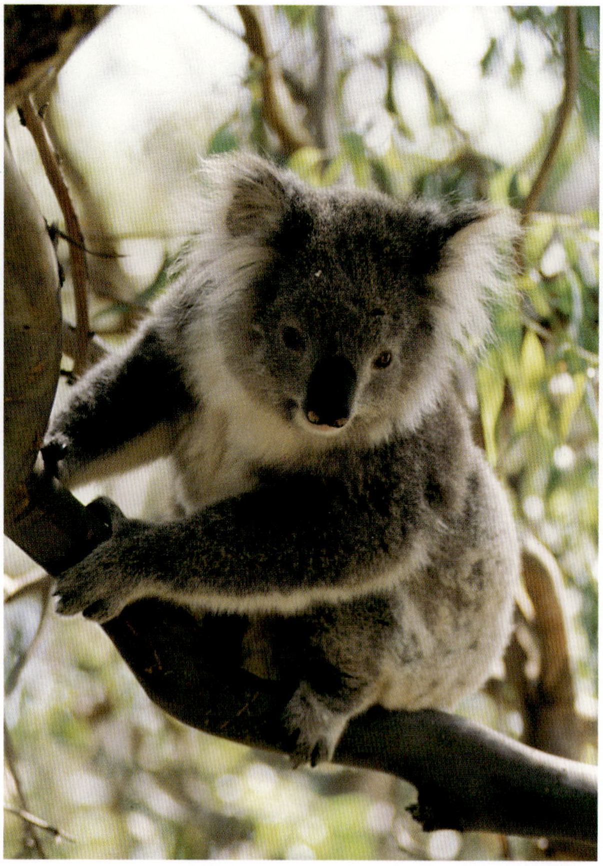
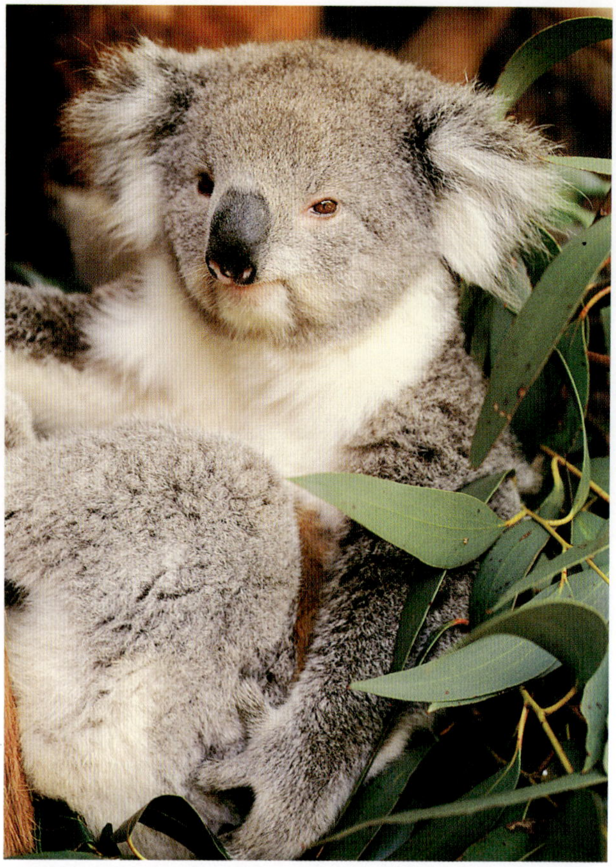
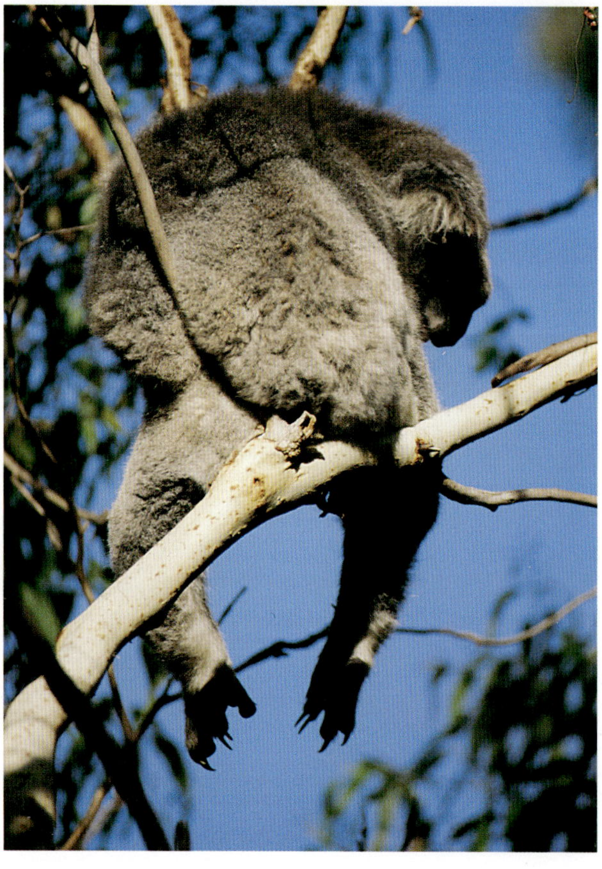
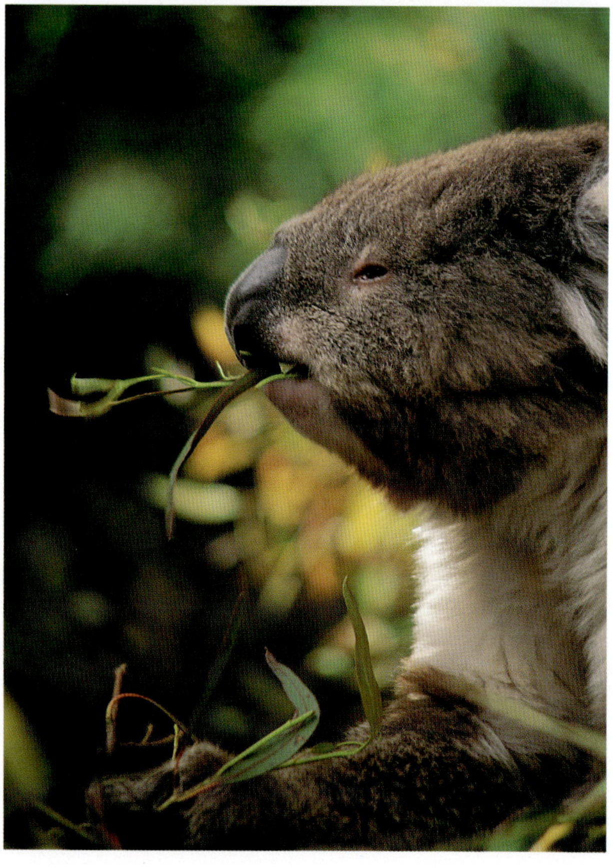

My home is in the eucalyptus trees,
which are necessary for my survival.
They give me shade, comfortable
branches to curl up on,
and, most important, leaves to eat.

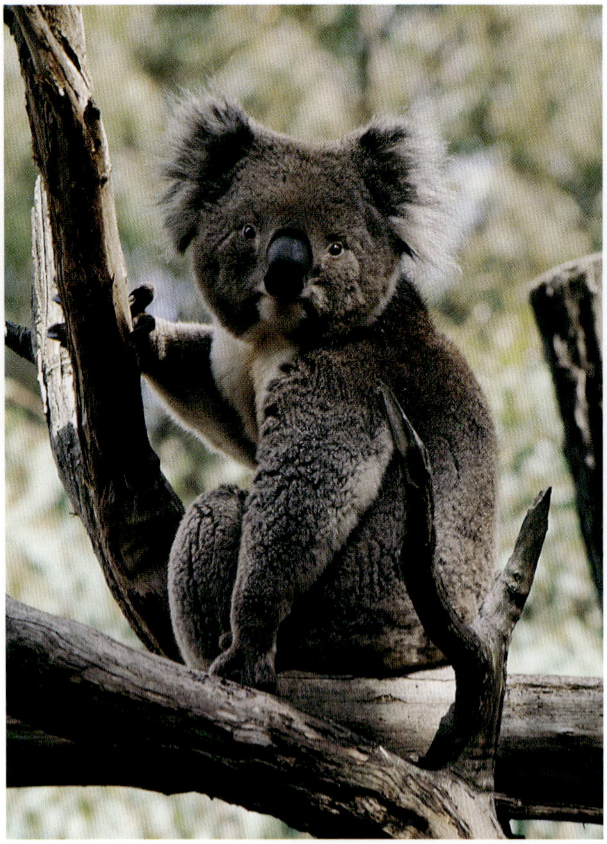
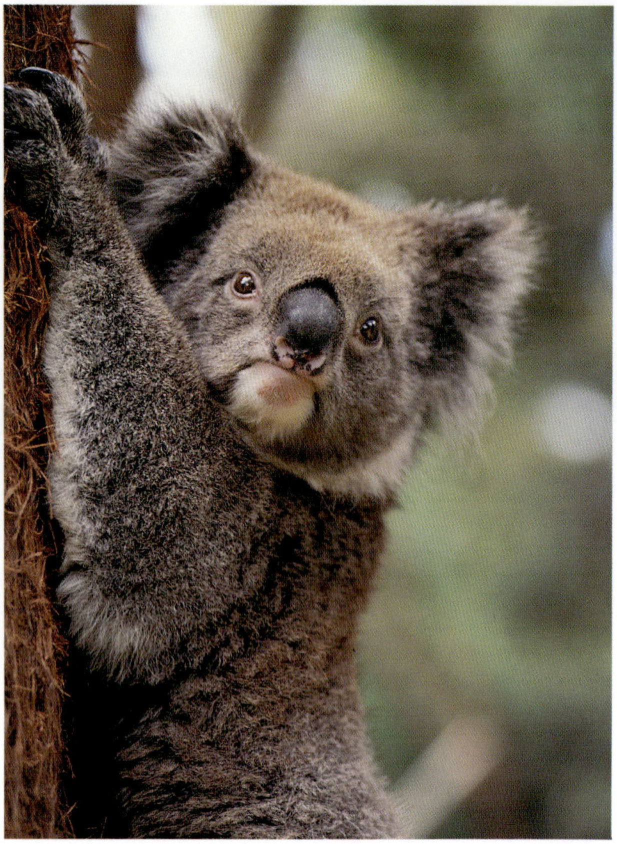
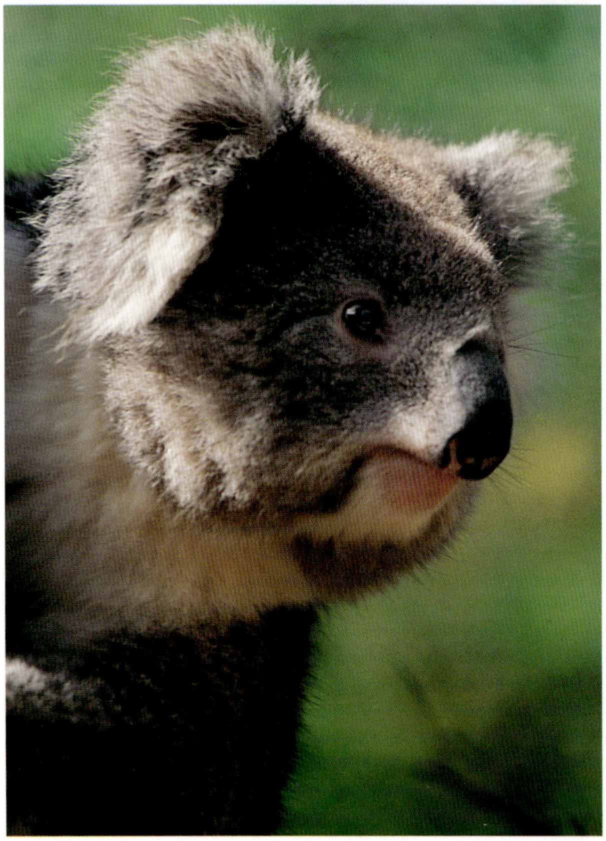
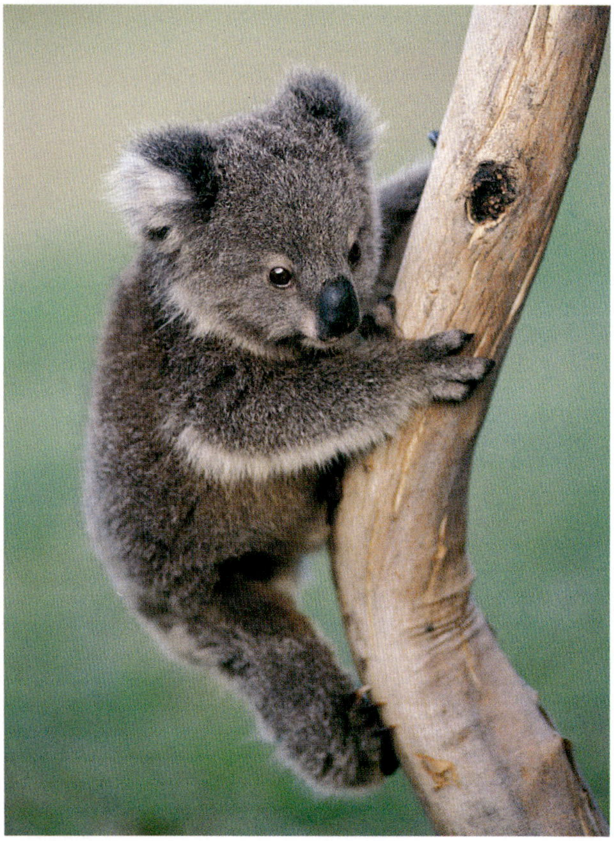

Some people think koalas are bears,
but that's not true at all. We are marsupials,
a primitive mammal with a pouch
for our young, similar to kangaroos,
wombats and possums.

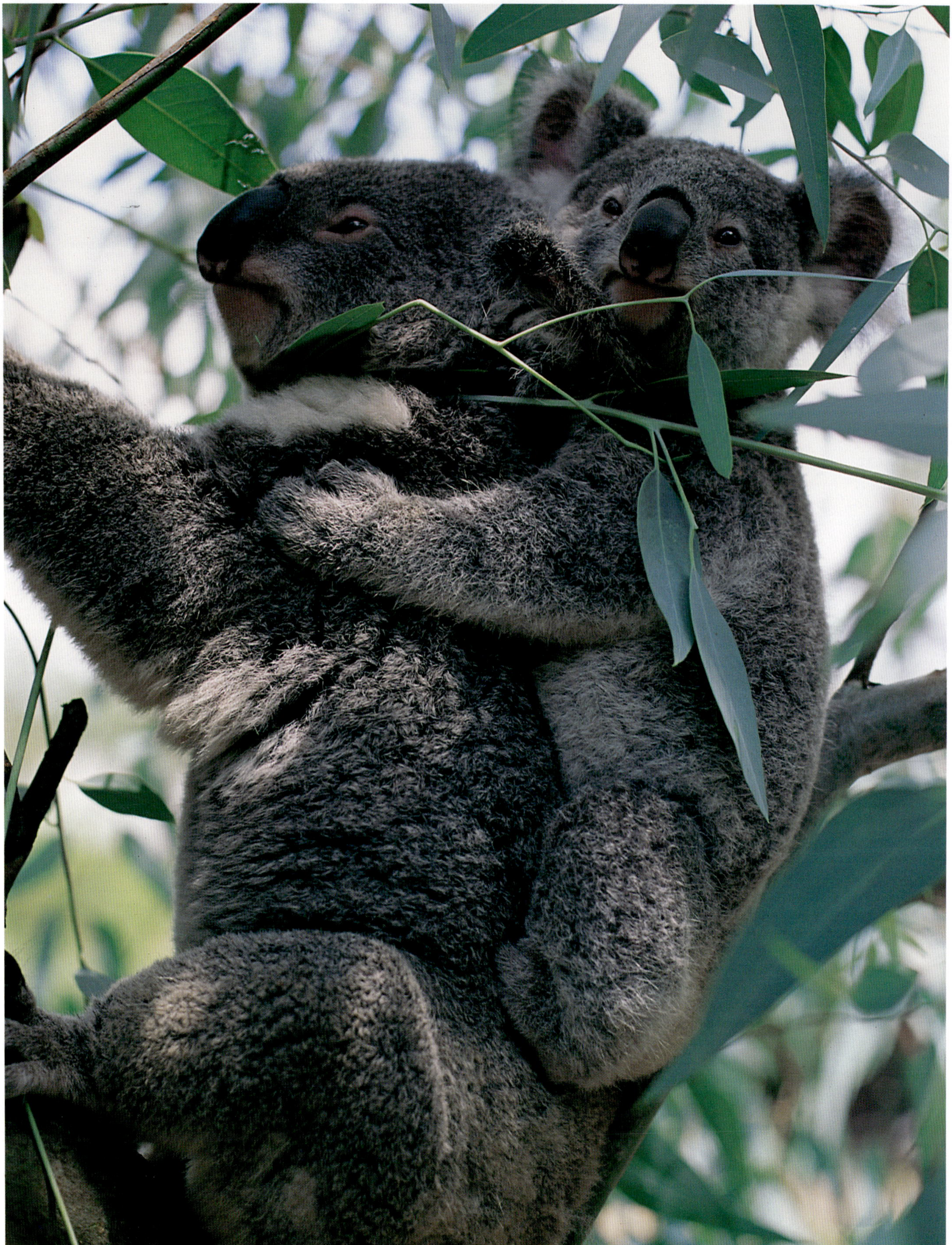

Meet Cuddles, my baby sister.
She's ten month's old.

Generally, koalas prefer to live alone.
My mother will look after Cuddles until
she's about one. Then they will separate.
At the age of around two, Cuddles will start
her own family. But for now she enjoys
riding on my mum's back - what fun!

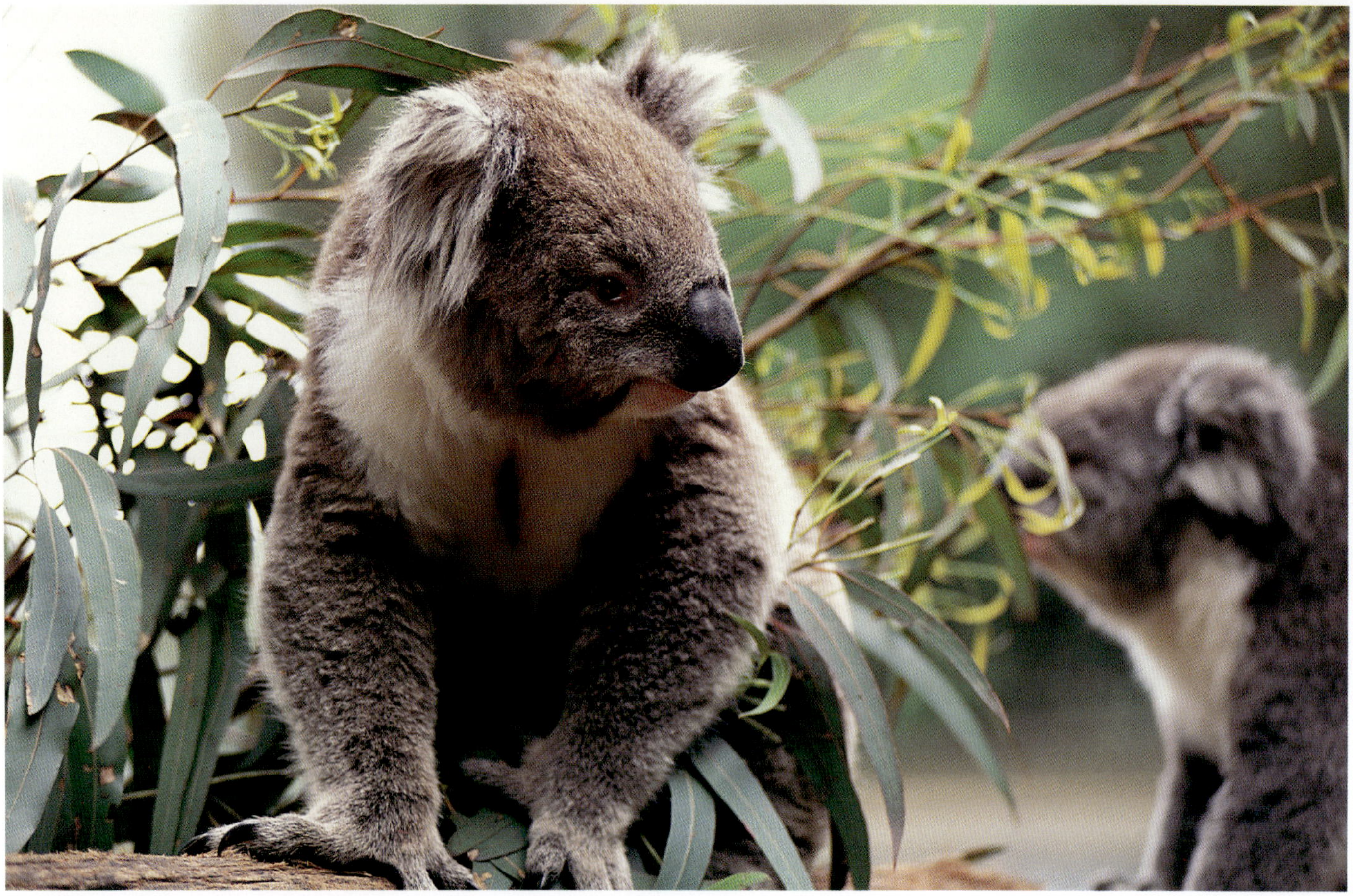

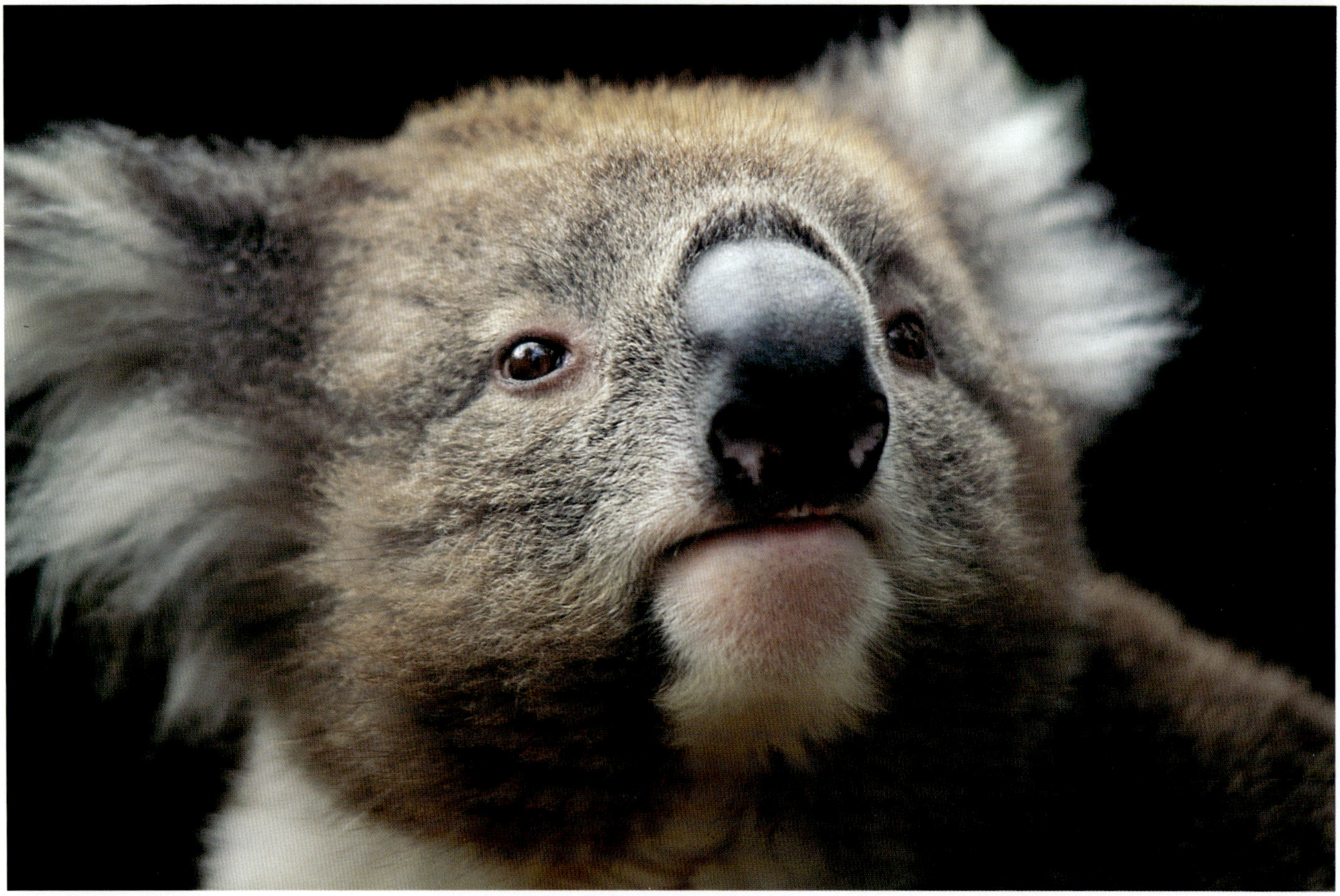

My daddy is nearly twice the size of my mummy and weighs about 12 kilos. He marks his territory with a smell by using the dark scent gland on his chest. Also he tilts his head back and makes loud "snore-belches" to let others know where he is.

12

When it comes to food, koalas are not as fussy as people think. We eat leaves and buds of over 120 varieties of eucalyptus trees.

Sometimes we feed on other trees like the golden wattle, coast tea-tree and cherry tree. Our total diet is only 567 grams a day, which is equal to a bowl of cereal.

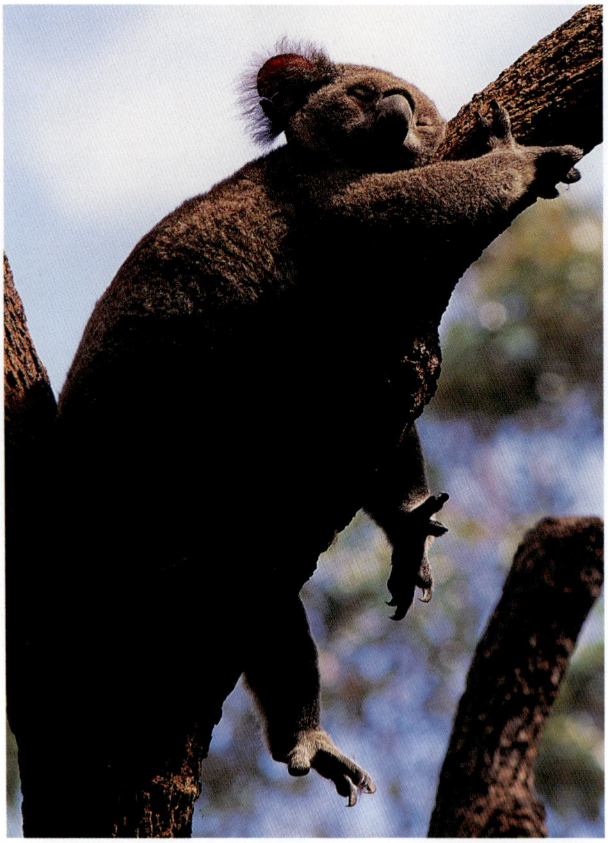
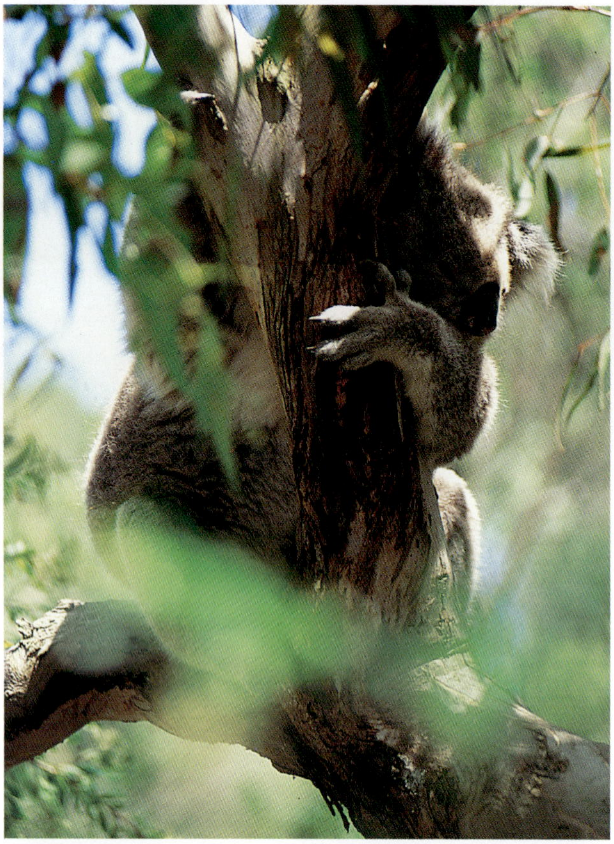
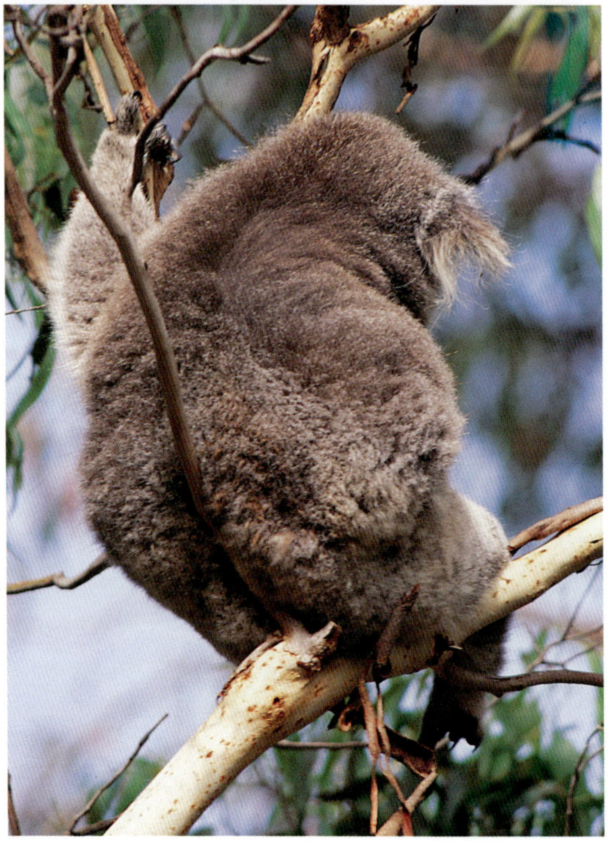
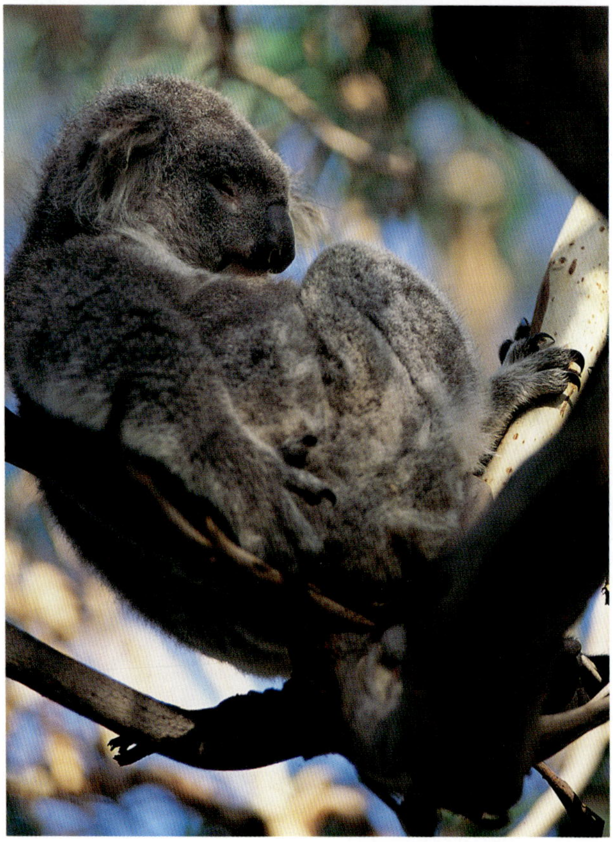

Koalas spend about 19 hours each day just sleeping and resting. The reason we don't have much energy is because we eat so little.

It has nothing to do with the chemicals in the eucalyptus leaves, which is just a myth.

In fact, we do lots of other things besides sleep, such as climbing and grooming.

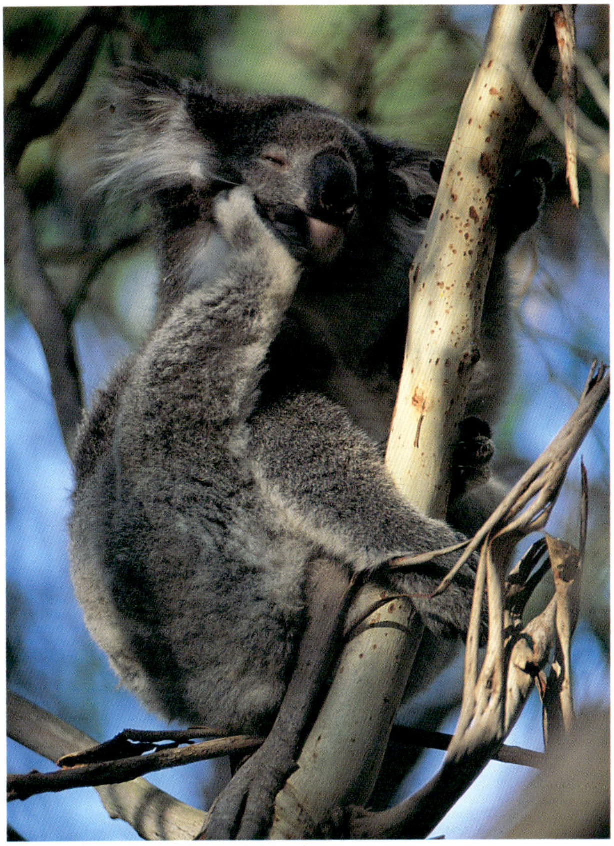
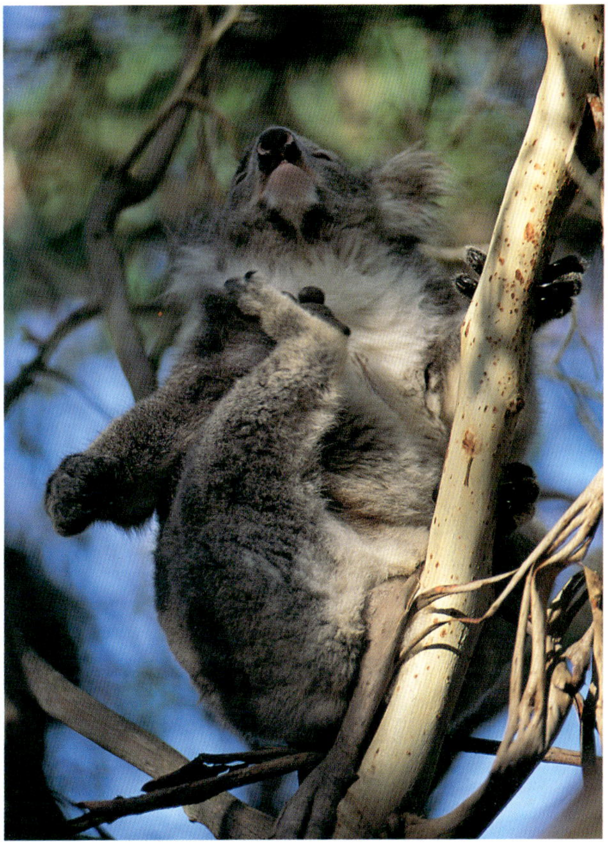
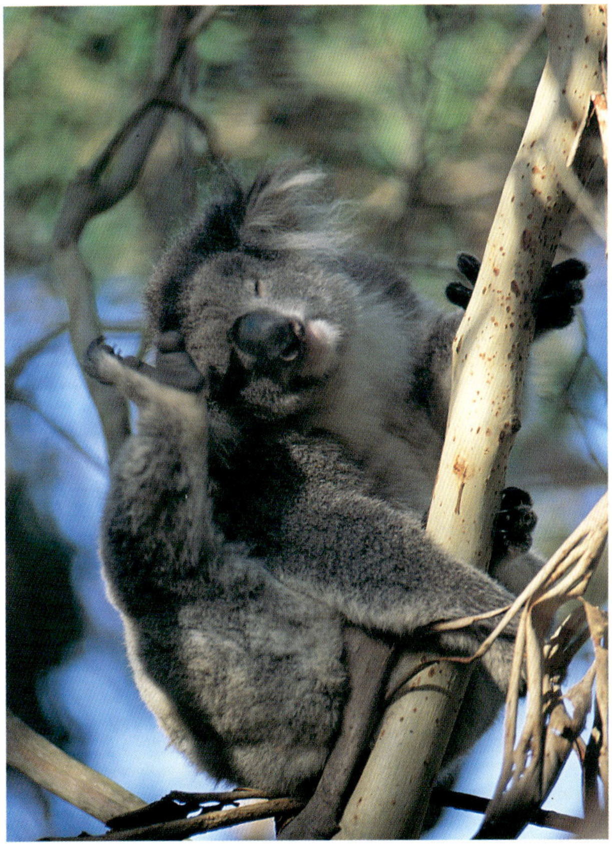
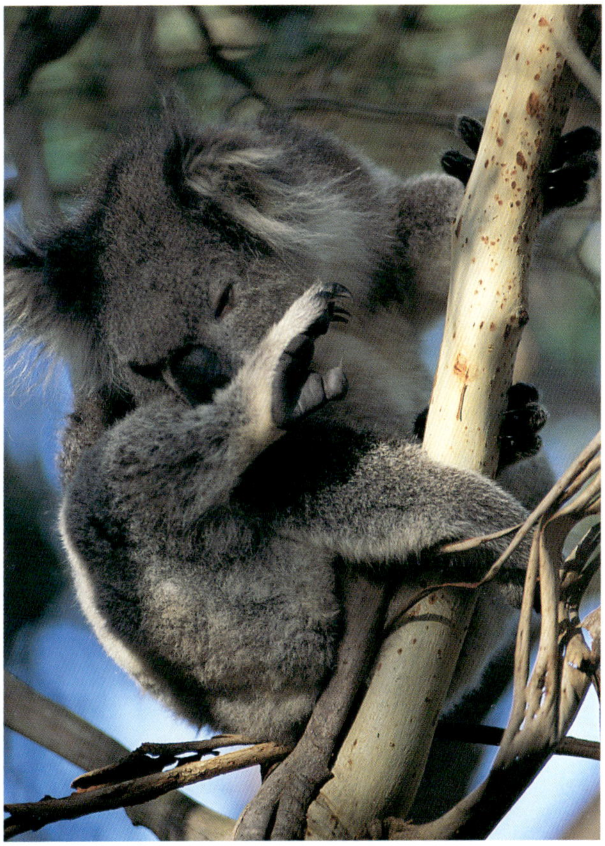

We walk on the ground...

...and even jump from tree to tree.

When you come to visit me, you can get a close look at my powerful hands and feet...

cute little nose...

sharp front teeth...

almond-shaped eyes...

...and fluffy ears.

Koalas can live to be around 15 years old.
There are about 80,000 of us left in Australia,
but every day our habitat is being destroyed.

Other dangers include bushfires, drought,
starvation and disease. And in the city areas
we are victims of dogs and cars.
We need help if we are going to survive.
I hope you care about us because
only you can make a difference.

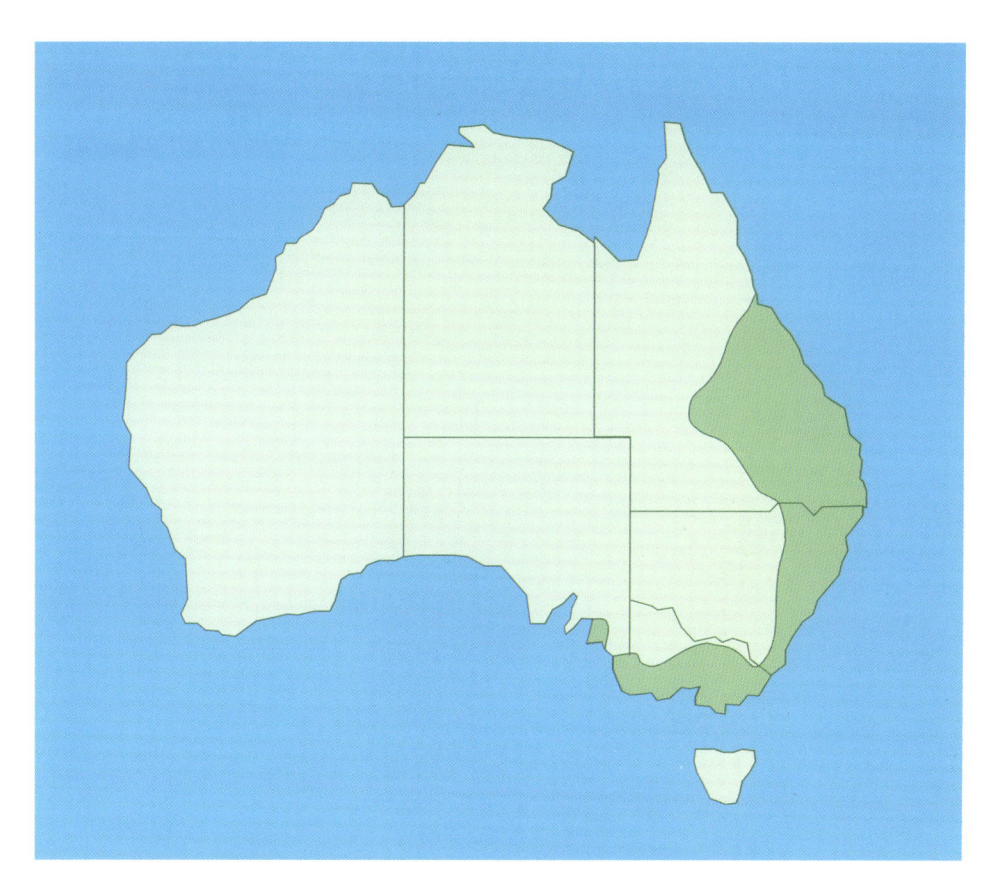

LOCATIONS WHERE KOALAS MAY STILL BE FOUND

KOALA FACTS

SCIENTIFIC NAME: Phascolarctos cinereus

HABITAT: Found exclusively in Australia in areas ranging from coastal islands to low woodlands. Since koalas depend on eucalyptus leaves for nourishment, they must be surrounded by various species of eucalyptus trees.

WEIGHT: Male up to 14 kilos and female up to 11 kilos.

DIET: Primarily eucalyptus leaves. The koala's digestive system is specially adapted to counteract the poisonous chemicals in the leaves. They also eat leaves from golden wattle, cherry, paperbark, and coast tea trees.

PREDATORS: Dingoes, dogs and foxes. Koalas became extinct in some areas of Australia in the 1920s because of over-hunting by man to supply the fur trade. Today, man is responsible for the ongoing destruction of the koala's habitat.

LIFE SPAN: Around 10 years in the wild, and up to 15 years in captivity.

NUMBERS REMAINING: Less than 80,000.

SUGGESTED READING

KOALAS Lynn M. Stone, 1990

KOALAS FOR KIDS Kathy Feeney, 1999

KOALA LOU Mem Fox, 1994

KOALAS: NATUREBOOKS SERIES
Sandra Lee, 1998

THE KOALA BOOK Ann Sharp, 1995

THE KOALAS OF AUSTRALIA
(Animals of the World)
Linda George, 1998

THE KOALA:
THE BEAR THAT'S NOT A BEAR
Diana Star Helmer, 1998

THE KOALA:
NATURAL HISTORY CONSERVATION
AND MANAGEMENT
Roger Martin, Kathrine Handasyde, 1999

Thank you for your interest in protecting the koalas. If you would like to help, please support the following organisations and wildlife parks.

QUEENSLAND

AUSTRALIAN KOALA FOUNDATION
Tel: 07 3229 7233
email: education@savethekoala.com
www.savethekoala.com

CARING FOR AUSTRALIAN WILDLIFE
Tel: 07 5543 5690
email: sharonwhite@ozemail.com.au

WILDLIFE PRESERVATION
SOCIETY OF QUEENSLAND
Tel: 07 3821 3006 and 07 3207 6339

WILDCARE - THE AUSTRALIAN KOALA
HOSPITAL ASSOCIATION
Tel: 07 5527 2444
email: wildcarevet@ozemail.com.au
www.wildcare.com.au

WILVOS
(WILDLIFE VOLUNTEERS ASSOCIATION)
Tel: 07 5441 6200
email: batmad@bigpond.com

LONE PINE KOALA SANCTUARY
Tel: 07 3378 1366
email: koala@koala.net
www.koala.net

CABOOLTURE SHIRE COUNCIL
KOALA COMMITTEE
Tel: 07 5420 0100
email: fitzgibbon@cabooluresc.qld.gov.au

KOALA ASSOCIATION LOGAN
Tel: 07 3290 4628 and 07 3808 7885
email: rcd@powerup.com.au

NEW SOUTH WALES

KOALA PARK SANCTUARY
Tel: 02 9484 3141
email: koalapk@ozemail.com.au

FEATHERDALE WILDLIFE SANCTUARY
Tel: 02 96221644
email: info@featherdale.com.au
www.featherdale.com.au

UNIVERSITY OF WESTERN SYDNEY
Tel: 02 4620 3203   email: r.close@uws.edu.au
Tel: 02 4620 3308   email:s.ward@uws.edu.au
http://fistserv.macarthur.uws.edu.au/
Biology/koala/kwatch.html

WIRES (HEAD OFFICE)
Tel: 02 8977 3333
email: wires@zeta.org.au
www.wires.au.com.

VICTORIA

BALLARAT WILDLIFE AND REPTILE PARK
Tel: 03 5333 5933 email: wildlife@cbl.com.au
www.wildlifepark.com.au

FRIENDS OF THE KOALA PHILLIP ISLAND
Tel: 03 5952 2407 and 03 5952 5497
email: jane.babbidge@dsto.defence.gov.au
www.vicnet.net.au/~fok

JIRRAHLINGA KOALA & WILDLIFE SANCTUARY
Tel: 03 5254 2484 email: tehree@jirrahlinga.com.au

WILDLIFE CARE NETWORK
tel: 03 9285 9453 and 03 5427 1352

PRYOR
Tel: 03 9722 1117
email: koala_watch@hotmail.com